GOOD DOGS

GOOD DOGS

Stories of Benevolence

Ruth Gordon

 Willow Creek Press

Published by Willow Creek Press
P.O. Box 147
Minocqua, Wisconsin 54548

Library of Congress Cataloging-in-Publication Data

Gordon, Ruth, 1925-
    Good dogs : stories of benevolence / Ruth Gordon.
        p. cm.
    ISBN 1-59543-597-2 (hardcover : alk. paper)
    1. Dogs–Anecdotes. 2. Human-animal relationships–
    Anecdotes. I. Title.
    SF426.2.G667 2007
    636.7–dc22
                                    2006102219

Printed in Canada

If there are no dogs in heaven, then when I die, I want to go where they went.

—Attributed to Will Rogers

Contents

Acknowledgments

Most stories in this book have come from dog lovers who want to share their experiences with delightful pets, service dogs, or the rescue of dogs who have needed help in the worst way.

The old gentleman, Archibald Dimitrios, delayed several suppers at Puerto Vallarta's Dot Com Café in order to tell the story of Lord Geoffrey, lying at his side.

My friend, Ann Long shared the hilarious e-mails from her daughter, Diana, about Ollie and the end of a human relationship but not of a dog relationship. Thanks to cousin Charlie and wife, Barbara, for sharing Harry with us. Teresa Davenport, Manager of Public Relations at the Seeing Eye, was kind enough to review my story of Morris Frank.

Marla Weiland Kohl invited me to her home so I could meet Daisy and watch her at work. Marla was also generous with her review of the manuscript.

Lisa LaVerdiere, executive director of Home For Life, gave me access to the many poignant stories of her residents. Officer Mark Ficcadenti, head trainer for the St. Paul Police Canine Unit, not only took the time to tell some of his experiences, but he clarified incidents that were not clear in the manuscript.

Introduction

Dogs, like people, live with unequal opportunities for happiness and good fortune. Some are born into hopeless situations while others are born into or find a good life. The world is full of haves and have-nots. The luckiest dogs have loving families. Our beloved golden retriever, Ben, was definitely a lucky dog. He had doting owners who trained him to be polite and from there on, we all had just plain fun.

Sadly, there are millions of unlucky dogs who suffer from being neglected and/or abused. It is inconceivable to me that a human being could abuse a pet, but of course it is also inconceivable that humans abuse one another. Psychologists tell us that behind an abused pet there may well be abuse among family members too. Domestic violence, child abuse, and pet abuse rarely occur in isolation from one another. In fact, both Maine and Vermont have recently passed laws to grant protective orders to pets in domestic violence cases.

But this book is about dogs, all kinds of dogs—some with careers, some who were abused and ultimately cared for, and some just plain loving pets. Each dog has his or her own story.

First, because of this author's bias, a brief word in defense of anthropomorphism is in order. Pet owners instinctively attribute human motives and feelings to their pets. They use words like *happy, loving, sad, mad*, or *frightened—words* we understand and feel. Critics of this approach use words such as *aggression* instead of anger, *maternal instinct* instead of affection, or *flight behavior* instead of fear.

Jeffrey Moussaieff and Susan McCarthy Deloacorti take a scientific approach to this debate by presenting a large body of research in their book, *When Elephants Weep, The*

Emotional Lives of Animals. The authors present convincing evidence that most animals demonstrate a wide spectrum of feelings. While an animal's vocabulary is not expressed in words, animals do express themselves in other tangible ways. They may whimper, groan, growl, cry in pain, shiver with fear, jump with joy, wag a tail, or purr.

Indeed, the authors contend that animals exhibit a much wider range of emotions than even the most observant human may realize.

The true dog stories in this little book reflect some of the researchers' findings. There are stories about dogs helping people and stories about people helping dogs. Either way, there is no doubt that meaningful relationships and strong bonds can be formed when communication is conveyed in words or in ways other than words.

Part I

People Helping Dogs

Lord Geoffrey

Lord Geoffrey

& Other Dogs of Puerto Vallarta

Every winter when we visited Puerto Vallarta, Mexico, we noticed an old man who walked down the uneven walks with a cane in one hand. In his other hand, he held a leash that was attached to a tall and very strange looking dog. Indeed, one had to take a second look to be sure it was a dog. This dog was long-legged, came almost to the old man's waist, and had a spotted brown and white coat with a definite look of mange. The dog appeared emaciated, resembling a greyhound in stature but with the colors of a dalmatian. He probably could have used a cane too because he walked with a limp due to a front leg and foot that appeared to have been broken and never set. His unique appearance made him one of a kind and definitely *not* a thing of beauty.

There were rumors about this pair: the dog was found in a garbage can with a broken leg; the owner sends to the United States for special skin medicine at a cost of $200 a month; and, the man was a Mexican mystery-story writer. I found it irresistible not to get the real story about these two so one day I approached the man as he hobbled down the street. Using my very best Spanish, I explained that I write dog stories and wondered about his dog. He smiled and said in perfect English, "For starters, let's try English." That squelched one rumor. While he spoke Spanish, he was definitely from the United States. After a brief conversation, he granted me an interview the next afternoon at the Dot Com Café.

When I arrived at the café, his dog lay on a blanket on the café floor while the man was eating a sandwich. He said he wanted to make one thing very clear first thing. Mexicans are accused of not loving their pets. This is not true. What visitors do not understand is that Mexicans must make financial priorities. What comes first? Is it food, clothing, books, and medical care for their families, or food and medical care for their pets? Tourists who leave their pets at expensive kennels while they travel do not understand what it is like to have to make such choices. As long as I understood this, he was ready to be interviewed.

Before learning about the dog, I asked him to tell me a little bit about himself. He seemed purposely vague about many details. However, he said his name was Archibald Dimitrios and that he preferred to be called Dimitrios. He had taught English Literature in California. Neither the school nor the city was named. His wife had died fifteen years ago. They never had children but it had been a wonderful marriage. Her death had been devastating. Dimitrios had apparently engaged in some self-destructive behaviors during the first few years after her death. He finally turned to writing, but he declined to give the titles of any of his books. When he moved to Puerto Vallarta, he met Lord Geoffrey, the dog lying at his side. He truly believes that Geoff and he saved each other's lives. It turned out that both the dog and Dimitrios had equally mysterious backgrounds.

His Lordship had been a beach dog although his physical appearance would refute that. Therefore, it is safe to say that, with Geoff's looks, he did not originate on the beach, even though that is where he was found. Dimitrios had once had a young neighbor who was dying of AIDS. This young man became very fond of a stray dog and put food and water out each night to encourage the dog to stay around. Dimitrios named this dog Lord Geoffrey because of the dog's hauteur and regal appearance. Dimitrios promised the young man that, after his death, he would take care of his dog, which he did. (Another rumor refuted: Geoff was not found in a garbage dumpster.) And the strangely bent leg? On close examination, it appeared that it was more likely a congenital defect, possibly a club foot.

His lordship appreciated his newly found good life, but he seemed to remember what it had been like to be homeless and hungry. One day Geoff saw a skinny beach dog hungrily eating a sandy piece of pizza. Another dog came along and tried to grab the pizza. Geoff broke away from Dimitrios, dragging his leash, and growled the interloper away. He even stayed around to make sure that the right dog finished the pizza.

Geoff showed a protective side on other occasions too. When he first came to live with Dimitrios, a beagle named Macho was also part of the family. When the three of them visited the veterinarian, Geoff watched out for Macho.

On one occasion, when Macho was being examined by the doctor, Macho let out a yelp. Geoff jumped up and got between the veterinarian and Macho. Dimitrios had to remove Geoff from the examining room so that the doctor could finish Macho's examination.

The old man and the old dog became inseparable through the next eight years. Dimitrios must have been in his late seventies and the old dog was probably the same age in dog years. They lived together, slept together, and even went to the doctor together. When Dimitrios went to the dermatologist, Geoff went with him, much to the dismay of patients in the waiting room. Both the dermatologist and veterinarian contributed their knowledge in treating Geoff's mange, eczema, and skin allergies. The medications were very expensive but they came from Mexico, not the United States.

One summer Dimitrios returned to the United States for two months. During that time, Jorge, a neighbor, took care of Geoff. Jorge owned a yellow taxi and liked to watch television. Consequently, Lord Geoff took up taxi riding instead of walking and spent a lot of time watching T.V. (Dimitrios did not own a television.) Geoff went with Jorge when he drove to the airport to pick up Dimitrios after his two month absence. When Geoff spotted his old friend inside the customs area, he ran through the gate, jumped up on Dimitrios, and gave him a very satisfying, wet welcome.

Once home, Dimitrios quickly learned that in order to keep his dog at home in the evenings, he had to buy a television set. In addition, Geoff decided that any yellow taxi would enjoy having him as a rider. Although dogs are supposed to be color-blind, one can only assume that Geoff either was an exception or that he had learned to read.

Because of Geoff's peculiar appearance, Dimitrios said that strangers in the street, especially tourists, often accused him of not caring for the dog properly. I had a first-hand experience with this attitude. One day I waited with Geoff outside the bank while Dimitrios did some banking. A passing tourist came up to me and said, "Isn't it awful the way they treat dogs down here?" I answered that this dog was probably one of the most loved and well-cared-for dogs I had ever known anywhere. "Really?" she asked skeptically. "Really," I answered. Just then Dimitrios came out of the bank and His Lordship wagged his very strange tail.

When we visited Puerto Vallarta last year, we learned that Geoff had died of old age. Dimitrios looked a lot older himself. His gait was even slower than it was the year before. He said he was very lonely without his beloved dog and the street of Olas Altas certainly looked different without the two of them walking together.

OTHER DOGS OF PUERTO VALLARTA

As serious dog people, my husband and I not only got to know Lord Geoffrey in our visits to Puerto Vallarta, Mexico, but we spend a lot of time dog-watching, more accurately dog-worrying. In a city where there are no humane societies or dog rescue groups, homeless and ownerless animals are very visible. With heavy hearts, we watch beach dogs as they struggle for survival, staying close to restaurants, garbage cans, and street vendors.

The balcony of our rented condominium faces the ocean beaches in one direction and in the other direction we look up the street named Olas Altas where several little sidewalk stands sell jewelry, dresses, food, belts, and bags. At night, alcoholics, drug addicts, and the mentally ill often use the beach as a place to sleep. For weeks, we watched one of these persons, a young man, lie under a few old thread-bare blankets each night. Cuddled up next to him was a young, possibly three- or four-month-old tan mongrel. When the man awakened each morning, the little dog jumped up, wagged his tail, and followed him wherever he went. Many days the little dog desperately clung to one of the man's legs with all four paws. The man would then walk along limping with the weight of the dog on his leg. It appeared that the lonely man and the lonely dog were meant for each other. Then, a month later, the man disappeared and the abandoned young dog wandered about forlornly, becoming just another beach dog.

We are not the only tourists who get concerned and emotionally involved in the plight of these animals. One dog-loving tourist bought a spaghetti dinner every night for the dogs she saw near her hotel. One evening we were walking along the beach just as she placed her plate of spaghetti out on a rock. She sat nearby watching two thin collarless

Beach dogs of Puerto Vallarta

mongrels share the plate. They did not fight over the food, nor did they gobble the food as one might expect hungry dogs to do. Rather, it seemed as if they knew that with their kind of hunger, they needed to eat very slowly to keep from getting sick. And eat slowly they did, seeming to savor every strand.

Many strays follow a step or two behind walkers on the beach. Are they hoping for a new owner, or a handout? While they seem hopeful, they also seem wary of a possible physical rebuff so they stay alert for any kind of approach, good or bad. Some dogs are pregnant and some have obviously given birth recently but there is no sign of puppies anywhere.

One late afternoon we looked down the street and saw two little boys playing catch with a small puppy while their father looked on laughing. We named this little creature Luckless. I wanted to run downstairs and offer a few well-chosen Spanish comments, but my husband's good sense prevailed.

The next afternoon I saw the puppy and the apparent owners while I was out walking. Close up, the puppy looked to be no more than three weeks old. When I approached them, I asked in Spanish, "How old is your little dog?"

"Eight weeks old. Do you want to buy him for one hundred American dollars?"

"No, because I couldn't take him home," I answered. "But he looks only about three weeks old. Where is the mother?"

Finally, the man said he was four weeks old and that the mother was at their house. He continued to try to sell the puppy to passersby as we chatted. Eventually, I broached the subject of the children playing catch with the puppy. "Wasn't that hard on him?"

"No, Señora, he likes it." Whereupon he picked up the little dog, raised him up in the air, and swung him around by his front legs. "See, he likes it." I told him I wasn't so sure and departed.

That night, sitting on our balcony, we watched the same little boys chase the puppy around the street. Suddenly, the little dog darted into a large storm sewer that led to the ocean. The boys lay face down at the edge of the sewer and tried to reach him, but it was too late. The puppy was literally washed into the Pacific Ocean.

Perhaps the awful end to this poor little creature's short life spared him a long difficult life. At least that is how I had to look at it in order to endure the sorrow I felt.

After this experience we found Lucy, the owner of Lucy's Cucú Cabaña, a little store that sells imported hand-made items, many with a humorous animal theme. She started a non-profit program that concentrates on spaying, treating, and adopting stray cats and dogs.

Her group of volunteers worked tirelessly trying to round up beach and street dogs. This is trickier than it sounds. A dog with a collar signals that there is an owner, so these dogs must be left alone no matter what their apparent condition. The volunteers, therefore, only pick up dogs without collars. However, it soon became apparent that some collarless dogs had owners and that a few abandoned dogs wore collars. Her workers had to be circumspect, diplomatic, and very careful not to antagonize or insult any possible owner.

Dogs with owners may lay lethargically outside their homes without a leash, rarely barking, and rarely wagging their tails. They may have a skin condition or fleas as they spend a lot of time scratching themselves. They seem indifferent to strangers passing by and none has ever given either one of us any cause to be fearful. As Lucy says, families will naturally feed, clothe, and medicate their children before they will spend money on the care of their dogs.

The goal of Lucy's organization was to de-flea, de-worm, and spay or neuter stray dogs (especially females who brought their puppies into a hostile environment), and then prepare them for adoption if possible. Lucy

organized fundraisers and held auctions of art-
work donated by local artists. Several veteri-
narians donated their services or worked at
reduced fees. Volunteers took some of the dogs
home and gave them regular food, water, and
exercise while they were receiving medical
care. Lucy also started an educational program
for the schools, teaching children appropriate
care and behavior toward family dogs. There
was a noticeable reduction of stray dogs on the
streets and beaches of Puerto Vallarta during
the seven or eight years Lucy devoted her time,
energy, and money to this program.

Unfortunately, her organization's non-
profit status was challenged so the program
was terminated. While other groups have tried
to take up the cause, none has been as effective
as Lucy's program.

My husband and I have come to fancy ourselves as expert dog observers and continue to
enjoy this pastime, filling in with our imagina-

tions when we have absolutely no facts about a particular situation. We rarely pass the corner of Insurgentes and Caranza streets without seeing a dog with a collar lying (apparently sound asleep) in front of a locked store. We speculate that the owners leave the dog to guard the store at night and when it is closed. All we really know is that day after day he lies sleeping in the same place every morning when we walk by.

In contrast, a little spaniel of sorts (the size of a cocker spaniel with the coloring of a Brittany) is just the opposite. He keeps himself busy all day. He goes to work each morning with his family, who are food vendors on the beach. In the heat of the day, he finds a shady spot from which he can keep track of his owners. When the family's mother goes home for a few hours during the day, the dog lies on the walk with his head resting on his front paws watching for her return. When he spots her coming at a distance, he jumps up with joy, runs to greet her, and runs back to work with her for the rest of the evening.

Our friends, Bob and Carolyn from Cincinnati, are fellow dog lovers and dog watchers. One day Bob had the good luck to spot two delightful golden retrievers playing on the beach. When he saw them, he dashed home and pushed Carolyn in her wheelchair to the beach where the dog owners insisted on carrying her in her chair to the edge of the ocean so she could play with Sandi, part golden retriever and part yellow Labrador, and Anejo, a full-blooded golden retriever. Regardless of their ancestry, they pass as twins. The dogs paced in the water with tails anxiously wagging and intently watching the hand with a ball in it so they could lunge into the water at the very instant of the throw. A "chuck-it" was especially appreciated because the ball went a greater distance. Retrieving and returning the ball for another throw was a joyful game for everyone.

The dogs often go to work at the sports bar owned by their human family. Anejo had his moment of fame in Puerto Vallarta when he was kidnapped outside the bar two weeks before Christmas. The owners offered a reward through radio announcements and posters placed in shop windows and on many cars. A week later Anejo was returned after the reward was paid. And who was the kidnapper? A policeman who said he knew that "gringos" adored their pets and would always pay a reward for their return!

Besides wearing a collar, what is the best way to distinguish a stray dog from a skinny family dog? I have my own way of telling the difference between a stray dog and one who has an owner. Because there are no dog ordinances or leash laws in Mexico, nearly all dogs run loose. Of course some owners do use leashes. However, among the unleashed dogs, strays have very definite characteristics. First, they act depressed. They are hungry, thirsty, and may have one or more untreated diseases so they lack energy. Second, they very rarely wag their tails, my barometer for a dog's mental health and general mood. They will not chase a ball or a frisbee, and they seem to be incapable of having fun. Third, they have "flat" personalities. They do not respond to human approaches and they do not make eye contact the way pets do. I have never seen a stray mongrel snarl or approach a human in a menacing way. They are simply unresponsive. And, it should not be surprising that most street dogs look remarkably similar. After all, they are all related—short tan hair, medium size, long legs, large pointed ears, and a long curved tail that never wags.

In contrast, when I see a dog running up and down the beach with a wagging tail, I know there must be a ball or Frisbee, and an owner, somewhere close by. The dog and owner are having fun. The dog feels good, has energy, and is well fed and watered.

One can hardly mistake a beach dog for one of these lucky dogs. We have a favorite group of lucky dogs. The owner has a dalmatian, a golden retriever, a german shepherd, and a tan furry little mutt, all off leash when they run the beach. The dalmatian always carries a stick and the little mutt stays at the heels of the golden retriever. The German shepherd carries a Frisbee that he likes to drop at the foot of a stranger, apparently wanting the Frisbee thrown, but when the stranger reaches for it, he snatches it away, playing "I'm quicker than you." One morning the German shepherd dropped the Frisbee on a sleeping beach bum who woke up startled to see a large canine nose nudging a Frisbee across his chest. It did not help his hangover.

Just before we left for home this year, I walked along the beach. Suddenly, I heard a young man snapping his fingers and calling, "Vamanos." I looked down and there was a puppy, three weeks old at the most, struggling through the sand. I stopped and just stared at him. The little dog came to my feet and squealed. I could not think of a single Spanish word so I shouted. "Carry him. He is too young." The young man picked him up and asked if I wanted him. I will always regret saying "No." However, without any dog rescue group available, I do not know what I would have done with him, but in retrospect, it certainly seems like taking him would have been the right thing to do.

Every year in the United States, millions of dogs are abandoned at the side of a road, at racetracks, and at animal shelters. However, the abandoned dogs in the United States are not visible on a daily basis like the ones we see on our visits to Puerto Vallarta. Our wonderful respite from winter in a paradise-like setting does not allow us to forget the great inequities of all lives, both human and canine.

Ollie

Ollie

"Hi Mom, guess what!" It was my friend Ann's daughter, Diana, who is studying for her master's degree in social work at the University of Wisconsin in Madison. "Guess what" always made Ann hold her breath.

"Dear, I can't imagine what."

"We adopted a stray puppy! But there is a problem," answered Diana.

Multiple questions came to Ann's mind so she took them one at a time.

"Who is *we*?" *We* turned out to be Diana and her boyfriend, Jake.

"Where does the puppy live?" She hoped Diana had not brought the pup to her dorm room. The answer to that question was a relief. "He lives with Jake in his apartment."

Finally, Ann gathered her strength and asked the question, "And what is the problem?"

"The problem is he has hip dysplasia of both hips and he can't walk... And he needs surgery right away... $1,200 a hip. What do you think Mom?"

"I think I am going to have to think and I think you and Jake need to think also. I will talk to you later. E-mail me the whole story. Good-bye." Ann sat down and wondered how much she should tell her husband, Elliot.

The next day Ann received a long e-mail. After reading it, she thought about the whole crazy story of the puppy they named Ollie, how they got him, how much they already loved the puppy, and how much the puppy loved them. They seemed to be committed to a strange little puppy who was in urgent need of a staggering amount of money.

First, the way they found Ollie turned out to be quite a story in itself. Jake and Diana were walking home from a movie one afternoon when they spotted a pack of four dogs in a park. They were roughhousing and running wildly about. Two of the dogs seemed to be puppies. The puppies also seemed to be the underdogs (an unfortunate descriptor) in a series of snarling exchanges. None of the dogs wore a collar so Jake and Diana, both ardent dog people, became concerned enough that they called the Humane Society on their cell phone. They decided to stay and watch these canine interactions until someone came to pick up the dogs. While they were waiting, one of the puppies left the pack and came over to sniff out Jake and Diana. The pup apparently liked what he smelled and Diana fell in love with him on the spot. He was pure white, had big ears that stood straight upright, and he had big brown eyes that spoke one thousand "I love you's." Suddenly, Diana looked at Jake and said, "You have to adopt him."

"What?" he said.

"You just have to adopt him. I've never asked you to do anything before, but you just *have* to adopt this puppy." She spoke with such urgency that Jake simply did not know what to think.

Just then the Humane Society personnel arrived. They asked for Jake and Diana's observations, then gathered up all the dogs, put them in their truck, and were about to leave when Jake said, "I would like to adopt the white puppy."

Burt, the Humane Society driver, told Jake and Diana the pros and cons of taking the dog right at that moment. If the dog went with Burt now, he would have a thorough physical examination and be treated for probable fleas and possible heartworm. In addition, his multiple dog bites would be cleaned and treated. This would save them some veterinarian bills. Since both Diana and Jake had college loans and were short on money, this free veterinary care was persuasive. However, there was a down side to having Burt take the dog now because the dog could not be released to them for adoption for at least eight days, which is the state law in Wisconsin. It gives an owner time to locate a lost animal and an opportunity to take it back. Diana and Jake decided to let the dog go with Burt, but they wanted it clearly understood that they wished to adopt the pup as soon as possible.

They walked home feeling like dog owners. Every day, either Diana or Jake went to the pound to check on Ollie. They were not allowed to see him because there was a rule that while a dog was waiting for the possible return to an owner, no prospective adopter could visit the animal. This did not stop them from going to the pound every day. At least they could find out if an owner had called and they also could receive a brief health report.

Diana and Jake counted the days and on the ninth day, they went to the pound, ready to adopt Ollie. Coincidentally, the owner also arrived on the ninth day, but fortunately he was too late. He was Spanish-speaking and so, it turned out, were some of the dogs! He wanted his dogs back. All of the dogs belonged to him and one was Ollie's mother, not a surprise because of her striking resemblance to Ollie. Had he been a responsible owner, he might well have been able to get his dogs back in spite of being a day late. However, the Humane Society made their decision on what was best for the dogs. The dogs were not registered and the owner violated a city ordinance by having more than two dogs living in his house. In addition, he was charged with animal abuse and neglect by letting the dogs run, and allowing them to have several unattended medical problems. The dogs were also underweight and undernourished because they had not been fed adequately. In addition, the Humane Society personnel wondered about the owner waiting to inquire about his dogs until the ninth day. The man claimed he loved the dogs, but he also said that he really did not have enough money to care for them properly. He was charged room and board for the eight-day stay for all four dogs and signed them over to the Humane Society.

Diana and Jake were greatly relieved at the outcome. They bought Ollie, and Jake took him to his second floor apartment. All of their limited spare time became devoted to their new puppy. While Diana speaks Spanish, Ollie only seemed to understand English. However, Jake speaks German and since Ollie looked more like a white German shepherd than any-thing else, Jake started to teach him German commands. Remarkably, Ollie learned to understand his new language in a short period of time. Ollie was now truly bilingual.

Ollie's fleas and dog bites healed up nicely with his new treatment and diet. The puppy was so much fun that they thought they would enter him in the Muttminster dog show in Beloit. However, after they had him for a few weeks, Ollie became lame. He had a great deal of trouble walking. He could not climb the stairs to Jake's apartment, and he was obviously suffering from a great deal of pain. Jake and Diana took him to a veterinarian who x-rayed him and found he had dysplasia in both hips. This is particularly serious in a puppy because he could become permanently disabled if the surgery is not done promptly before there is further bone growth. The doctor prescribed an anti-inflammatory pain killer to make Ollie more comfortable while the young owners figured out how to raise the $1,200 for each hip surgery. Ollie responded well to the medication. He seemed more spirited and happier. He was even able to jump on the sofa so he could look out the window whenever either one of them drove away.

Jake and Diana were determined to raise the money for the surgeries. Jake worked for a bar in Beloit. The bar owner suggested having a benefit at the bar to raise money for Ollie's surgeries. Diana and Jake thought that was a great idea and everyone went to work. Diana and Jake made posters that were put up throughout the town. The bar put out big brandy glasses for donations. Even a small local band volunteered their services. With the Ollie benefit planned and in place, the first surgery was scheduled for October 13th.

On the afternoon of October 13th, Ann received the following e-mail: *Jake just got a call that Ollie is done, and that the vet said his surgery was 'uneventful'. This is relieving. He may be able to come home as soon as Friday but he will be a tri-pod for a few weeks. The bad news is that Ollie's whole upper right thigh is shaved, and he will be wearing a lamp-shade (better known as an Elizabethan collar) for at least three weeks. This will make for dif-ficult cat-chasing, and the other dogs might pick on him. Ollie's benefit is this weekend. (Donations are always welcome—thanks to sister Barb already.) I am bogged down with school work. Back to the grind. Love, Diana*

The next day Diana received $100 from her mother with a note, "Don't tell Dad."

The day after that, Diana received $100 from her father with a note, "Don't mention this to your mother." Only $1000 to go for just the first surgery!

On October 18th, the parents received the following e-mail: *Ollie's benefit went really well. Including parental donations, an anony-mous $100 (we suspect it came from Ollie's vet because he came to the benefit), the cover charge at the door, the jar at the bar for a week, and cookie sales, we made around $1200. This covers the entire first surgery, x-rays, meds, and a little more. Ollie came home* *on Friday. His right cheek has no fur. He is putting weight on his leg already, which the doctor says is a good sign for quick recovery.*

When Jake went to pick him up after his surgery, Ollie acted like he didn't even know Jake and that his only best friends were the vet and his aide. He has since come around, and is more affectionate than ever. He likes to have his butt covered with a blanket and he sits on the couch with his head in our laps. He is capitalizing on his condition by crying if his rawhide slips off the couch so we have to pick it up for him. However, when there was a pizza in the living room, the hand of God lifted him from the couch and his legs began to work again. That's all for now. Love, Diana

For almost three weeks, Jake had to carry Ollie up and down the stairs to his second floor apartment, which had to be done at least four times a day. The dog was growing fast and weighed 65 pounds by then. Not only that, but the lampshade was huge, making it very awkward for Jake to get all of Ollie securely in his arms. Jake was relieved when the lamp shade came off and this three-week routine was over. Ollie seemed delighted also.

At Christmas time, Diana, Jake, and Ollie came to Minnesota for a visit. It was then that I had the opportunity to meet Ollie. He was without a doubt one charming fellow and now one year old.

He had the extraordinary energy of a young dog. He was also very shy. When I entered the house, a white streak flashed by and into the kitchen. As I passed the kitchen door, a white cocked head peaked around the door to get a better look at the stranger. In a matter of minutes, he came out slowly and cautiously, smelled the back of my outstretched hand, and then accepted a nice scratch around the ears. Diana demonstrated his language skills. He obeys commands readily in both English and German.

The second surgery was delayed and surprisingly, may never have to be done because correcting the first hip greatly improved the other hip. However, if the second surgery should have to be done at some time, the bar owner has volunteered to do another benefit for Ollie. The first event not only brought in some new business but it gave the bar a new image as a community benefactor. Everything was on track. Then in the spring, Ann got another one of those telephone calls.

"Guess what, Mom?"

"I just can't guess anymore."

"Jake and I have broken up."

"But what about Ollie?"

It turns out that while the romance did not last, Ollie's life is going great. So far, he does not need the second surgery and he is living the life of Riley with Jake. His favorite occupation is relaxing in the hammock in his back yard.

*Romeo**

The names in this true story have been changed by request.

Romeo

Betty Close from the Minnesota Golden Retriever Rescue Association received an anonymous telephone call. The caller said that a six-month old golden retriever was living in a closed garage twenty-four hours a day. She said that a bowl of food and some water were placed inside the door most days but the dog had not seen daylight for weeks. In addition, the dog had given up whining for human attention weeks before.

It is frustrating that so many of Betty's calls are anonymous because it makes it much more difficult to investigate when the facts are apparently hear-say and often difficult to verify. However, Betty went to the home to investigate the situation. She was able to diplomatically negotiate with the owner and convince him that in the best interest of both him and the dog, the dog needed to live elsewhere. When she went to the garage, she found a depressed puppy that had given up trying to interact with people.

When she carried the pup to her car, he brightened up a bit to find himself in daylight. She took him to one of the rescue families for care and assessment of the impact of his previous environment.

The rescue family immediately named him Romeo because he was so loving and grateful for his new life. He quickly learned to play, run, and fetch balls. He was easily house trained. He was friendly with strangers and all of his pent-up frustrations seemed to come out in positive rather than negative ways. He seemed to have no retaliatory behaviors, and best of all, he was deemed very adoptable.

An older couple, Hannah and Joe Hansen, came to visit him. They had recently lost their pet and were ready for adoption. It was mutual love at first sight. The Hansens loved golden retrievers and Romeo was a beauty. Romeo greeted the Hansens as if he had known them forever. He wagged his tail constantly while he gave both of them a very thorough sniff test. He also kept raising his paw to show them his only trick. Of course it was more than a trick; it was a gesture to entice the beginning of a touching relationship. After the hand/paw shake, he rolled over on his back, the sure sign of trust, to get a good belly rub.

Needless to say, he went home with the Hansens that afternoon. He was assured that his second life would be idyllic. They bought a nice big round dog bed that was placed between Hannah and Joe's recliner chairs. They snoozed together. They watched television together. And they meditated together while they watched the evening fires fade. He loved their long slow walks together. Indeed, it seemed as if he wanted to be with them every moment. However, three things disturbed him. They were all related to darkness.

Romeo refused to go to the basement if there was no light on; he would never get in their car if it was in the garage; and he moaned all night long. Hannah came up with an intuitive solution for the latter problem. He was afraid of the dark even in his new house so they bought a night light. They left it on all night. Romeo never moaned in his sleep again. Romeo's love and gratitude knew no bounds.

Sailor

Residents at Home For Life

Home For Life, located on forty acres of land in western Wisconsin, is a non-profit sanctuary where loving, lifetime care is given to special needs animals, mainly cats and dogs. Their residents cannot be adopted because of age, disability, medical problems or behavior issues. However, they live active lives in keeping with their individual problems. Dogs and cats live amicably in housing that has heat in the winter, air conditioning in the summer, and music at night. Dogs have daily walks and exercise, and veterinary care is available around the clock. In addition to providing a sanctuary, the organization has partnered with programs for victims of family violence, at-risk teens, and senior citizens. The dogs for these community programs are carefully selected and go through basic obedience training before they start special training for their particular jobs.

The poignant stories of these residents speak to the success of their program as well as the resiliency of the canine spirit when love and care are given even after years of devastating cruelty. Many of the dogs who come to Home For Life, and similar organizations throughout the country, are broken in both spirit and body. It takes time before a troubled animal can learn to trust human beings. A few, of course, never reach a degree of trust that would enable them to cope in social situations. The people who rehabilitate them not only go through training, but also have special personal qualities. Dedicated volunteers are always an essential part of the staff.

Dogs come to rescue groups, no-kill shelters, and foster homes from a wide variety of sad and tragic circumstances. Some are surrendered by guardians because of a death, illness, or divorce. Unfortunately, many are simply abandoned. The animals arrive bewildered and frightened. Some have lived under horrific circumstances that often include deprivation of water and food, physical abuse, and confinement. These dogs are usually suspicious of people, expecting no different treatment from their new caretakers than what they experienced previously. Their fears may be expressed in aggressive and self-protective behaviors. It takes patience, individual assessment, and trial and error interventions to make changes in their trust level for behaviors to change.

The dogs' behavior toward humans is not the only consideration. Their behavior toward other dogs must be given attention too. Dogs do not like every dog they meet. Therefore, finding compatible dorm or house mates can also be a challenge. The goal of the sanctuary is to give each resident a secure, happy, and purposeful life. Here are the stories of a few of the canine residents from Home For Life.

SAILOR

Sailor came from a not uncommon circumstance: being kept tied to a tree, a light post, or a fence for 24 hours a day. In Sailor's case, his elderly owner claimed to love him. However, from the age of six weeks, Sailor, a border collie, lived at the side of a road tied to a 20-foot chain for three years. His only shelter from the Florida sun was a cardboard box. The owner lived with a sister who did not like dogs. She not only refused to allow Sailor in their yard but even refused to have him anywhere near their property.

Sailor's constricted life in the sun was made even more miserable because he was regularly taunted by children and sometimes physically abused with sticks and rock throwing. Occasionally, Sailor worked himself loose, but someone always seemed to bring him back to his chain instead of to a place where he might have gotten help.

Through the years, Sailor's mistreatment made him more and more wary of people and he became very protective of what little space he had. His loving nature was sorely challenged. He was poked at and taunted with broom and mop handles. In order to protect himself from these assaults, he learned to growl in a menacing manner whenever someone approached too close to his space. Sailor gained a reputation for having unpredictable behavior. This in turn created more abuse by those around him. He was hungry, miserable, and underweight. He became known as a "pest" and "nuisance." Finally, after many complaints, Sailor was confiscated by the authorities.

At the animal shelter, Sailor was placed in a cage. He was judged to be a "good" dog. Possibly, he was better off in a cage. At least he was not being teased and abused. However, his owner came to get him, agreeing to treat him humanely this time. Eventually, the owner abandoned the dog because he could not afford or was unable to fulfill the requirements of the authorities. Once again, Sailor was brought back to a cage at the shelter, but this time it was because he had finally bitten a child who was taunting him. As a result, he was declared unsuitable for adoption and slated to be put down.

Home For Life was told of Sailor's plight. Their personnel indicated they would take Sailor so his life was put on hold, so to speak. It took almost four months to complete negotiations for his release from the pound. When Home For Life was finally permitted to accept legal responsibility for Sailor for the rest of his life, they had him transferred to a veterinary hospital. He was found to be underweight and infested with heart worm. He was treated for his illness and given nutritious meals. After two weeks of medical care, Sailor started to respond to loving humans and was ready to be moved to the Home For Life sanctuary in Wisconsin. Volunteers went to Florida to get him.

Sailor now lives happily with other dogs. He loves his own fluffy bed. He enjoys being petted and of course he loves to run across his huge yard, something very special for him. The remarkable thing about Sailor is that he is a gentle, loving dog who seems to have the ability to put the first three years of his life behind him, something not all abused animals can do.

Because the problem of chaining up dogs is nationwide, various communities are working to curtail the amount of time a dog can be restrained. Research has demonstrated that chaining dogs for long periods of time not only creates aggressive behavior but is closely related to serious biting incidents. People for Ethical Treatment of Animals and Dogs

Deserve Better are two organizations that are promoting ordinances to restrict how long a dog can be tied up. In St. Paul, Minnesota, the following animal ordinance was passed in 2004: *Animals cannot be restrained by a chain, tether or other tie-out device to any stationary object for more than two consecutive hours without at least a two-hour rest or relief period between each chaining. There may be exceptions for properly designed pulley and kennel systems. Violators could face fines ranging from $50 to $300.*

The ordinance is too new to know if it will have the effect of actually reducing the problem. However, St. Paul citizens who see incidents of prolonged chaining, similar to Sailor's case, will at last be able to obtain legal action by reporting such cases to the local animal control agency.

MOPPET

Moppet is a three-year-old, tri-colored basset hound with soulful eyes and especially long tan ears. One summer day, Moppet's owners found her lying by the side of the road near their home. She had been hit by a car and was unable to walk.

They immediately took her to their veterinarian who prescribed steroids to see if that could reduce the inflammation and restore her mobility. However, there was no improvement, and Moppet was also incontinent. Because the young family had a new baby and very limited income, they surrendered Moppet to Home For Life where their Emergency Medical Care Fund paid for an evaluation at the University of Minnesota Veterinary Care Center. Moppet had x-rays and an MRI with the hope that her condition could be identified and corrected by surgery.

Sadly, there was no way to fix Moppet's

Moppet

paralysis and incontinence, but she now lives a quality life. At Home For Life, she has her own custom-made wheelchair, which is actually a two-wheel cart attached to her back legs. She gets around by pulling herself with her two front legs. She has excellent front body strength, a lot of energy, and a very cheerful nature. She has very good mobility and even keeps up with her roommate, Sailor, the border collie, who runs with the wind.

When she is not using her cart, Moppet wears socks and "muttluks" that protect her skin when she drags her body along. Her run is covered with rubber cattle mats to protect her skin further. Moppet and Sailor make a visitor feel very welcome when they come to greet you at their yard.

NIKE AND MEAGAN

Nike and Meagan are two lovely dogs with nothing in common except that their former owners visit them on a weekly basis. They are among the animals in the Home For Life Angel Care program, which provides affordable care of pets when an owner can no longer provide that care at home.

Meagan was a 14-year-old chocolate Labrador who had worked as a guide dog for thirteen years. Her human partner adored her. Meagan faithfully led her owner to work at Ecolab in St. Paul, Minnesota. Meagan endeared herself to the coworkers in the office. She especially delighted in those who provided her with her favorite treat, popcorn. Meagan's presence brought special joy to all the employees who knew her. Unfortunately, this 13-year partnership had to be ended because Meagan developed medical problems and became arthritic. Her partner spent months searching for a good home, but no one wanted an old dog with medical problems. The thought of putting her down was unthinkable. Eventually, Meagan's partner heard about Home For Life. She brought Meagan to investigate the possibility of staying there. It looked like a good fit so Meagan moved in, and her bills were even paid by Ecolab.

Meagan

The arrangement worked out beautifully for Meagan. She missed having a job, but she found a new one. She was very fond of cats, having lived with three during her guide dog years. She became the official greeter for the feline leukemia building. Meagan's life was very satisfying. She had a new job, loving new friends, lots of exercise and good food, and best of all, her partner visited on a regular basis. Indeed, she visited Meagan just a few hours before she died at the age of 15 years and seven months.

Nike is now over a year old. She is an Alaskan Husky who had some trouble controlling her back legs at about eight months of age. She, her mother and siblings had been chained up and used as bait dogs for pit bull fighting practice. She was the only survivor of her

Nike

canine family and was brought to Homeward Bound Rescue, which adopts out their dogs. She was adopted by a loving family. She chased butterflies in their yard, played with other dogs in an off-leash dog park, and just seemed to smile all the time.

Unfortunately, her problem extended to her bowel and bladder, making her incontinent. The new owners took her outside on a regular basis and got her a doggy cart, which she loved. With the wheels working far better than her back legs ever did, she ran with other dogs for the first time. She smiled more than ever too. However, the incontinence began to require more care than the working family could manage. They loved the dog and did not know where to turn. Nike was enjoying life way too much to be put down. Finally, they took her to Home For Life to see her reaction. She took to the barking greeters and the staff immediately. She adjusted very quickly. Her human dad visits her regularly and much to his relief, she is not upset when he leaves. That is because Nike knows he will come back soon with a new toy, an old shoe, and a treat. Their bond has been preserved.

Owners of dogs in the Angel Care program usually pay for their animal's upkeep. This program is also open to anyone who wants to include a pet in his or her will in order to assure that the pet receives good care after death.

LACEY, SCARLET, AND POLLY

Lacey, Scarlet and Polly all have a lot of enthusiasm, an outstanding characteristic of their breed, Shelties. With these three sisters, that's a lot of enthusiasm.

They came from "Punky's Refuge," a shelter run by a woman who developed physical and mental health problems, and could no longer cope with her situation. At the time of her death, more than 28 dogs and livestock

Lacey, Scarlet, and Polly

were found on her rural property in serious conditions caused by neglect. The woman's family decided to have the animals killed so that they could more easily sell the property. A group of concerned citizens became aware of this plan and with their own money, obtained a legal injunction to prevent the family from proceeding with euthanasia. The court allowed the volunteers to take charge of the animals.

A Wisconsin breed rescue group took the dogs, mostly shelties, and sought homes for them. Homes were found for all but Lacey, Scarlet and Polly. The three were very timid and shy, and their coats were matted and covered with dirt and excrement. In addition, Lacey and Polly are deaf. They have blue eyes and Scarlet has one blue eye and one brown eye. (Interestingly, blue eyes in dogs can be a tip off to hearing problems.)

The volunteers who rescued the dogs discovered that the three sisters were very bonded to one another. If separated, they cried until they were reunited. When together, they stayed so close to each other that they seemed to move as one dog. The other problem with this trio was that they had obviously been abused because they were very hand shy. When they saw an extended hand, they would duck, cower, and try to get away.

When the three arrived at Home For Life, Candy Nash, HFL's dog groomer, was immediately summoned. She had to shave all three because the neglect had left them with so much filth and matting that it was impossible just to groom them. Besides, their skins were covered with infected sores. Once they were clean and had daily care, they settled in very well. While they are still shy with people, they like to play with some of the other dogs. Lacey especially likes to pull Tuffy's tail (a terrier mix house mate). She of course cannot hear Tuffy's yelps. Lacey may be the youngest and is the most amenable to human contact. She was even able to participate in the Renaissance Program, a program for at-risk teens attending an alternative high school in River Falls, Wisconsin. She worked with a young girl who was afraid of dogs. Both the girl and Lacey gained more confidence, and Lacey obtained her Canine Good Citizen certification.

By now they all have beautiful coats that are kept clean and shiny with regular grooming. Polly may be the smartest of the three but she is also the most sensitive one. Besides being deaf, she has a deformed eye. Scarlet, probably the oldest, has had the most trouble overcoming whatever harsh treatment she had in her past. She is a gentle soul but stays timid when approached by people. She enjoys her sisters, though, and when you enter the grounds of HFL, these high-energy sisters make sure they are noticed even if they do not want to interact with you.

MEGAN

Megan is a slightly overweight female golden retriever. When I visited Home For Life, she caught my eye right away because I am very partial to goldens and was particularly interested in why she was there. Megan has her own little house and when she sees visitors coming, she almost strains her back wiggling with excitement. She passes much of her time watching a gopher dig a hole as he comes and goes up and down his underground home right next to her house.

When Megan is allowed off her front porch, she rushes to the hole and sticks her head in as far as she can. She comes up for air for a minute and then sticks her head back in the hole. It is very frustrating not to be able to see down there, but she keeps trying as her head fits in the hole almost up to her eyes. It makes me want to get a flashlight to help her.

Megan came to the attention of the Golden

Retriever Breed Rescue and a local vet. Because she had reportedly bitten a former family member, the rescue group did not want to put her up for adoption. However, the veterinarian's evaluation showed her to be an intelligent and kind-hearted dog. He recommended giving her a second chance.

It seemed likely that her previous owners had treated her very roughly in disciplining her when she exhibited her natural and youthful exuberance. In another instance, she had bitten someone during play that had gotten overly rough and out of hand. Dr. Petra Mertens, a behaviorist at the University of Minnesota Veterinary Teaching Hospital, felt that Megan was a dominant dog, but had a good heart. HFL decided to give her one more chance.

While at HFL, she has received gentle and consistent handling along with weekly basic obedience training. Her novice level obedience training made her a reliable citizen for staff to

Megan

handle. She was a great hit during her nursing home visits and can participate in the Senior Outreach Program.

According to the Center for Disease Control, 4.7 million people are bitten by dogs each year and most of these people are under 12 years of age. While there are vicious dogs that need to be kept away from the public, there is a need to educate children about their interactions with dogs.

In April, 1999, a seven-year-old girl, Kelly Voigt of Palatine, Illinois, was attacked by a dog. She had severe lacerations and needed over 100 stitches. This traumatic experience left her with post-traumatic stress syndrome and depression. Ultimately, she required help from a psychologist. After several months, Kelly and her psychologist decided she was an expert on prevention of dog bites and that she could share her experience with other children. Kelly and her mother met Nancy Skeffington, a school psychologist who had a Delta trained therapy dog, a golden retriever named Casey. Together, they started Prevent the Bite, Inc. For three years they gave presentations to the second graders at a local school. Kelly tells the children to remember the WASP steps., which are: 1) Wait—never rush up to a dog whether you know him or not; 2) Ask permission to pet the dog—this is important because some dogs do not want to be touched by strangers; 3) Stop, even if you know the dog, and let the dog sniff the top of your hand with your fingers curled inward—never show your palm; 4) Pet then and only then. Kelly's program ultimately received national attention. She has appeared on both the Today Show and Oprah Winfrey's show.

Kelly's non-profit organization has a web site: www.preventthebite.com that lists some excellent resources. Her simple message can prevent others from having a traumatic experience like hers. If Megan's owners had had this training, she just might be living with a family.

Ronnie

Ronnie

I first met Ronnie (Ronald of Gray Dawn, his A.K.C. name) when he was seven weeks old. My aunt and uncle had gone searching for a collie puppy, and when they found one with the same last name as theirs (Gray), they knew they had found their "meant-to-own" dog. In addition, one of Albert Payson Terhune's 1920s books about collies was titled, *Gray Dawn*. They liked to think that Ronnie's blood was really very blue.

I was fortunate enough to live close to my aunt and uncle so I had the joy of being part of Ronnie's life from the cradle up, so to speak. I helped with his toilet training by running him outside the minute he had swallowed his last bite of supper. He and I chased balls and sticks almost every day. His preferred toy was a long braid of my old nylon hosiery, good for a game of tug-of-war as well as just plain chewing. Learning to play like a puppy with a puppy when I came home after eight hours of nursing sick people could not have been a more joyous way to unwind.

Ronnie was a quick learner. When we walked, he was one of the few dogs I ever knew who grasped the idea that heeling was better than pulling. In just a few days, he learned all the "come," "sit," and "stay" of basic obedience school. Indeed, he never went to obedience school because he never had to.

Ronnie grew into a magnificent Lassie look-alike. He had beautiful penetrating eyes, a white blaze on his forehead, a white throat, and his body was covered with long silky caramel-colored fur. He was a gentle soul. He enjoyed interchanges with other dogs, cats, babies, and even tolerated young children who pulled his tail or ears. He did have one quirk, however. He snarled and became threatening toward any man who came to the door dressed in any kind of a uniform. No one could think of any unpleasant experience that might have caused this behavior toward people in uniform. Nonetheless, he terrified uniformed people and it was clear that he needed to be isolated when the postman, milkman, or iceman came to the house. He literally had a change of personality when he saw a uniform. My uncle had an offbeat way of thinking about this. He decided that this behavior was due to an ancestor becoming so frightened by a Scottish Queen's guard led by a large parading bagpipe band that the uniform fear had come down through his genes.

Ronnie learned to swim in the St. Croix River and he enjoyed his summers there immensely. He would have made a fine rescue dog because when any of us went swimming, he first tried to bark us back to shore. If that did not work, he swam out to escort us safely out of the water. All in all, he had a very good life and he gave all of us great joy.

When Ronnie was about three years old, my aunt became very ill with a rare disease, scleraderma. This is the disease that can be harshly described in lay terms as "turning to stone." For five years, Ronnie stayed at my aunt's side, watching over her when she coughed, laughed, cried, cooked, napped, or took a short walk. He was a loving gift for her through those years, and he adopted the role of devoted caregiver very naturally.

One spring my aunt and uncle put Ronnie in a kennel and drove to Mexico to fulfill my aunt's long desire to see Mexico's varied landscape and culture. On the third day into the mountains, they stopped at a little inn. My aunt lay down for a nap and never woke up. The small village had no mortuary or cremation facilities, so my uncle had to put my aunt in the back seat of his car and drive to the U.S. border. His son, my cousin, met him at the border, arrangements were made, and the two of them drove back to Minnesota together.

When Uncle Jim arrived home, he asked me to get Ronnie from the kennel. When I arrived at the kennel, I explained to the owner what had happened. After expressing her sympathy, she directed her concern toward Ronnie and how he would deal with the death. First, she asked me if the dog would know me because that was critical to his first sense of well-being as he left the kennel. Because my aunt had been the one who had brought him to the kennel before the trip, she thought this was particularly important. I assured her that Ronnie would know me.

We walked out to Ronnie's kennel, she opened its gate, and Ronnie came bounding out to greet his familiar family member with so much enthusiasm that he almost toppled me over. The kennel owner said that was a good start. Then the woman said that Ronnie would be very upset when he arrived home and discovered that my aunt was not there. She instructed me to make sure that Ronnie slept with a piece of my aunt's clothing for as long as he wanted.

When we arrived home, Ronnie greeted my uncle with great enthusiasm. Then suddenly, we could see he was bewildered. He left the living room and did what can only be described as a room search. First, he went through the first floor—kitchen, pantry, dining room, study. Then he went upstairs, stopping at every bedroom and bathroom. Finally, he came back downstairs very slowly after he had not found who he was looking for. He came into the living room where the family was gathered, he lay down, put his head on his paws, and searched everyone's face. When he received no encouragement, he closed his eyes, but it was obvious he was not asleep. His fruitless search was beginning to have its impact on his soul.

That night, my uncle gave Ronnie one of my aunt's sweaters. Rather than sleeping in his own place, he took the sweater, jumped up on her side of the bed, and slept next to my uncle for over a week. Then he went back to his own sleeping place downstairs, but he kept her sweater with him for another few weeks. Like all of us, he finally was able to let go of his grief, but it is doubtful, also like us, that he ever forgot her.

When summer came, my uncle moved to his cabin on the St. Croix River but he commuted to his office in St. Paul each day. Ronnie rode along joyfully. Later in the summer, my uncle had a rider, actually two riders. One was his friend, Betty, and the other was her large standard poodle, Cocoa. Ronnie was very put out about losing his front seat and being relegated to riding in the back seat with Cocoa. In fact, he was so put out that he constantly tried to push his way as a third passenger into the front seat. One morning Betty became so exasperated that she shouted, "One of these dogs has got to go." Ronnie got back into the back seat and never tried to ride in front again. As Betty said, dogs have a bigger vocabulary than we ever credit them.

Eventually, Betty and my uncle started a blended family of four. Because they decided to live in Ronnie's house, Ronnie made sure that Cocoa knew who was alpha dog. When Betty and my uncle had a cocktail before dinner, Ronnie snuggled up to my uncle and Cocoa sat next to Betty. When I visited and was disloyal enough to pet Cocoa, Ronnie immediately bristled and put his long imposing nose between my hand and Cocoa. Cocoa always got the message and moved away. Ronnie would give me a "How could you?" look and, in fact, did manage to make me feel a bit guilty for just patting Cocoa's head.

As long as both dogs lived, those were the house rules imposed by Ronnie. Neither should consort with the other's owner and neither dog was ever seen consorting with one another. In addition, they made it clear to their humans that they would never become friends.

Since both Betty and my uncle worked, the dogs were left to roam the neighborhood (before the leash laws) during the day. Neighbors reported that they were inseparable during the day. One was never seen without the other, but the minute the humans entered the house, the stand-off resumed. Their friendship was their secret.

The secret was out, however, the day Cocoa was killed by a car as he darted into the street in front of the house. Ronnie was inconsolable. For over a week, he sat in the back yard and made loud moans of grief day after day. It was the second time that Ronnie had lost someone special. Just a few months later, Ronnie died from a liver disease. He had never regained his former energy after Cocoa's death. One can only speculate that Ronnie's grief had a great deal to do with his own death.

Part II

Dogs Helping People

Buddy, the first guide dog in the United States

Morris & Buddy

The Incredible Guide Dog

During the 1920s, *The Saturday Evening Post* ranked among the most influential "home and family" magazines in the United States. It is hard to grasp that in the days before the internet, television, and only a few radios, magazines were the most important means of communication.

This story begins with an article in the November 5, 1927, issue of the *The Saturday Evening Post*. It was titled "The Seeing Eye." The author of the article was a wealthy Philadelphian, Dorothy Harrison Eustis, who had moved to Switzerland where she was breeding German shepherd dogs, mainly for the Italian and Swiss police. Her article described a school in Potsdam, Germany, where German shepherds were being trained as guides for German army veterans who had been blinded in World War I.

Across the ocean in Tennessee, this article was read to a wealthy and angry young blind man whose name was Morris Frank. His mother had been blinded in an accident and as a little boy, Morris had helped his mother, especially when they traveled. He did this in spite of the fact that he himself had lost the sight of one eye when a protruding tree branch struck him in the face while horseback riding. Then at the age of sixteen, he lost the sight in his other eye after a trauma when wrestling and sparring with friends.

Morris abhorred being dependent on people to get around and the idea of using a dog's eyes excited him. The more he thought about it, the more determined he was to get such a dog. He wrote to Mrs. Eustis describing his situation. It took a lot of persuasion but his perseverance induced Mrs. Eustis to let him travel to Switzerland and learn how to work with one of her dogs. In return, he promised to teach others to partner with dogs when he returned home. The outcome of this decision would affect the lives of thousands of blind persons for decades to follow.

For Morris, Mrs. Eustis had hoped to buy an already trained dog from the Potsdam School, but the school did not wish to sell any of their dogs. Therefore, she needed to train one of her own dogs for this young man. Fortunately, she already had just the person on her staff, Jack Humphrey, a trainer and breeder who had developed a rating system for predicting a dog's successful training. Teachability and endurance were high on his list of attributes for prediction of desired outcomes.

When the nineteen-year-old Morris arrived in Switzerland, he was assigned to Kiss, a female German shepherd chosen because she had "nerves of steel," an essential quality for what would become the first successful guide dog in the United States. Morris disliked the name "Kiss." When he first met this young dog, he told her that Kiss was no name for a dog and immediately changed her name to "Buddy." They then went to work.

Jack Humphrey, the trainer, was both stern and a perfectionist. For five grueling weeks, dog and man learned to work as one. Instructions were endless. "Stand tall." "Lighten your grip on the harness." "Let the dog lead—don't interfere." "Don't get in front of her." "Use hand signals and words for right and left." "Praise her." They walked miles every day. Morris often ached all over, but at the end of each exhausting day, he fed, watered, and groomed Buddy. Exhaustion ultimately turned to exhilaration. Morris and Buddy finally mastered their lessons. Morris was proud and they were ready to return home.

According to Peter Brock Putnam's book, *Love in the Lead*, Morris had been made over. "He was scarcely recognizable as the pale boy with hanging head and drooping shoulders" when he arrived in Switzerland on the night train from Paris. When he left Switzerland for home, "He walked with his head erect, chest out, shoulders square. His voice rang with new confidence and his smile was radiant." Buddy and Morris were definitely ready to start their work as a team back home. Humphrey's final words were, "Remember, don't let anyone touch or speak to the dog while she is working in harness."

Buddy became an instant celebrity among the passengers on the voyage returning home. Morris was exuberant when they arrived in New York, where they were met by a group of reporters at the dock. Morris boasted that Buddy could take him anywhere. A very skeptical (and possibly sadistic) reporter challenged his claim. With bravado, Morris accepted the man's challenge. Buddy and Morris were taken to West Street at the end of the docks. Fortunately, Morris did not know that West Street was also known as "death street." As Buddy and Morris started across the street, there were speeding trucks, roaring cars, horses, horns, screeching brakes, and shouts from drivers. After what seemed an eternity of stopping and hesitating, Buddy got Morris safely to the other side of the street. Greatly shaken, Morris said emotionally, "Atta girl, Buddy." Nothing in Switzerland had ever prepared Buddy to navigate traffic like West Street, yet she did it. They were indeed ready to show the U.S. what a guide dog was all about.

For years, Buddy and Morris traveled to every state, giving demonstrations to show the value of a guide dog for the blind. Mrs. Eustis did the same trying to raise money to start a guide dog school in the United States. As they convinced others that a guide dog could bring new independence to a blind person, they also opened the door for such dogs to have access to trains, buses, hotels, and restaurants. They lobbied for the legislation that allows guide dogs to go in public places, leading the way in later years for other assistance dogs to have the same access to public places. For Morris Frank, it was a crusade and Buddy, his steadfast partner, never failed him.

At one point, Buddy was diagnosed with kidney disease. He was treated by the veterinarian, Dr. Mark Morris, who used a special low protein recipe of a measured mix of dry cereals, cottage cheese, minerals, and meat. Because Morris Frank could not see to mix the ingredients, the veterinarian's wife canned the recipe for Morris in her garage. The success of this treatment became so well known that Dr. Morris eventually founded Prescription Diet® pet foods because he could no longer handle the increasing volume of orders from his home.

Together, Morris Frank and Mrs. Eustis endured many set-backs from skeptics, especially from professionals working with blind persons. They faced untold financial hurdles. The difficulty of finding and training instructors was described by Mrs. Eustis as their Achilles' heel. Ultimately, they were able to start The Seeing Eye organization, which held its first class in 1929. Now located in Morristown, New Jersey, The Seeing Eye is a canine training and breeding center where hundreds of blind people come each year to obtain a dog and to learn how to work with their assigned dog. It is interesting to note that Mrs. Eustis unceremoniously and with neither explanation nor apology took the name, Seeing Eye, from the Bible. "The seeing eye and the hearing ear, the Lord hath made even both of them" (Proverbs 20:12). The efforts of these pioneers have certainly been well served by the choice of just two words from scripture.

Puppy raising programs, the instruction of trainers, breeding programs for finding the best performing dogs, and training of human partners have now become very sophisticated because of decades of experience and research. Many other schools have been established across the country*. The thousands of well-trained blind person/dog teams that freely enter restaurants, theaters, hotels, buses, and airplanes today exist because of the perseverance of the pioneering efforts of Dorothy Eustis, Morris Frank, and the five-star German shepherd named Buddy. We can all say, "Atta girl, Buddy."

*An excellent resource for locating guide dog schools is www.deltasociety.org

Daisy

Marla and Her Hearing Dog, Daisy

Daisy certainly had never thought of having a career. After all, she had always lived with Hank, a well-known street person on Payne Avenue in St. Paul, Minnesota.

But one day Daisy and Hank's other dogs were gathered up in a big gray truck. The driver, a city dog-catcher, had a bit of a run trying to gather up all four of them, but he was eventually successful. He drove the dogs to a large building and put each of them in separate cages. The dogs missed Hank but the animal shelter was not all that bad. Daisy had regular meals. There was always water in her bowl and there was a roof that kept out the rain, wind, and snow. There also seemed to be a lot of people poking Daisy's belly.

The next thing Daisy knew, she was having pains and then five little ones were crawling all over her and demanding milk. She was a good nurturing mother until the pups got bigger and disappeared one by one.

What next? Daisy was spayed. That was not pleasant, but afterwards Daisy enjoyed all the people talking and playing with her as they assessed her for intelligence and friendliness. Now the people around her needed to know how she would do in a home environment. After all, she had never been inside a house. Daisy did not quite understand all the attention from so many people, but she rolled with what was given her as she always had.

Finally, Daisy took her first ride in a regular car. When she got out of the car, she quickly figured out how to climb her first stairs and then stepped into the first house she had ever entered. Daisy learned that her food and water bowls were always in the same place. She learned where to go to urinate, which meant she had to learn how to ask to go outdoors. Her foster parents learned that Daisy was friendly, intelligent, and an amiable learner. Her breed was of course a mystery, but most likely she had some border collie and husky in her; what else was anybody's guess. Nonetheless, she passed all her first tests and was deemed a good candidate for becoming a hearing dog.

Daisy was placed with Marla Wieland, a teacher of deaf children in Duluth, Minnesota. At age four, Marla had lost her hearing after contracting spinal meningitis. Through the years, Marla learned sign language and lip reading. Having once had hearing, Marla's speech is easily understood by hearing persons. While she was growing up, family members alerted Marla to sounds that needed her attention. As an adult living alone, Marla depended on mechanical devices and flashing lights to alert her to sounds, but she had no way of knowing when a fire alarm went off. She wanted a hearing dog if for no other reason than she knew that hearing dogs had saved the lives of many of their partners by alerting them to fire alarms.

When Daisy first came to live with Marla, they bonded quickly. They went to obedience school together. After all, a good career dog must be polite in public. They must learn to sit, stay, lie down, come, etc. Hearing dogs usually learn both hand signals and verbal commands. Daisy not only learned her manners but she was voted the most outstanding student in her class.

Next, Daisy needed to learn how to become a hearing dog. She had to learn sound training. This entails learning to alert a partner when there is a knock at the door, the ring of a telephone or doorbell, the sound of an oven timer, smoke alarm, radio or alarm clock. They also learn the names of family members. The

Hearing Dog Program in Minnesota trains their dogs in the deaf person's home. For over three months, a trainer came to Marla's house to teach Daisy the sounds that she must communicate to Marla. Together they practiced and practiced. Marla gradually learned she could trust Daisy to come to her and take her to the source of significant sounds. Daisy proved her knowledge when she awakened Marla at 3 A.M. one morning, alerting her to the fire alarm that Marla certainly would have missed.

Daisy even alerts Marla to new sounds that Daisy never heard during her training. For instance, while visiting Marla's sister, Daisy took Marla to the clock that was chiming. On another occasion, Daisy took her to a neighbor's apartment because of loud music. She also showed Marla a window where someone had thrown an object against the glass, and she even alerted her to a tornado warning siren once. She also lets Marla know when people just walk by her house, especially if the walkers have dogs. When Daisy took her Hearing Dog Certification Test, she passed with flying colors.

When Marla was asked about the down-side of having a Hearing Dog, the only thing she could think of was taking walks on cold winter days. She added that having a Hearing Dog is just all positives. It's good exercise. It's good to have a pet to come home to. It's a secure feeling to know that she will be informed of sounds happening around her.

Soon after Daisy completed her training, Marla and Daisy were invited to the Duluth Lions' Club for lunch as honored guests. Here Marla received Daisy's I.D. card and orange leash and orange collar, the approved public identification of hearing dogs at that time (now you will recognize hearing dogs by their blue and red jackets). Daisy was officially a service dog, eligible to enter public places. There was applause in the "hearing way" of clapping hands and in the "deaf way" with hands waving above heads. In spite of all the noise and commotion, Daisy stayed calm because she felt safe with Marla beside her and apparently these sounds did not seem to be ones she needed to tell Marla.

Daisy has also learned some sign language. She recognizes the commands 'sit', 'down', and 'outside'. She also recognizes the signs for 'eat' and 'cookie'. For a friend, she will sign back by lifting up her paw.

Daisy's life has certainly changed. She has gone from a street person to a career dog. She has learned how to do a rewarding job and she has found a wonderfully loving and dependable partner and home.

In 1996 Marla married Todd Kohl and moved to New Hope, Minnesota. Todd is also a non-hearing person so they took Daisy on their honeymoon in northern Minnesota. It was cold, so cold that Todd built a fire in the fireplace. Soon Daisy nudged Marla who was a bit baffled by her behavior. All Daisy did was stare at the ceiling. Marla soon realized that Daisy was looking up at a fire alarm. The chimney flue was partially closed!

One night during their honeymoon there was a loud thunder and lightening storm. Todd quickly learned that Daisy is terrified of storms. She gets up on the bed and shakes the bed vigorously as long as any thunder lasts.

Three years later, Marla and Todd had their first child, Alex. An important task for a hearing dog is to alert a partner whenever a baby cries. Marla did everything to try to teach Daisy to do this but Daisy stubbornly refused. Daisy had been an "only child" too long to encourage Marla to take any more time with the baby than she already did. When their daughter, Maggie, was born two years later, Marla had no more success in alerting her to the baby's cries. However, now that the children are a little older, Daisy is right on the job. When the children fight downstairs, she gets Marla to stop such goings-on. Both children have hearing and know how to sign so Daisy's help with the children now that they are older is important. Marla teaches English and reading to high school students so the children use day care. Daisy greets everyone when they come home. She of course is also a beloved pet.

Daisy is getting a little gray in the muzzle, but she is still a model hearing dog. She has had to make a lot of adjustments in her life, but she always comes through with flying colors. Daisy's rags to riches life is a tribute to her devotion and generous heart—and to her high career standards!

Harry

Harry

A Beloved Pet

Harry, a handsome, hyperactive yellow Labrador, charged into this world as an all around klutz with a wonderful sense of fun. No one knows much about the first three months of his life because my cousin, Charlie, found him at the St. Paul Humane Society for Companion Animals. However, it was known that in his short life, he had already been returned to the society twice. Two families had given up on making this canine delinquent a companion animal.

Charlie is a person who cannot live without a dog. His life is just not complete without a dog at his side. There is a large body of research that affirms that a pet, especially a dog, improves both physical and psychological health. Pet therapy in hospitals and nursing homes often has remarkable results on patients. In any case, Charlie's affection for his dogs is the embodiment of what a dog can do for a human.

When Charlie arrived at the Society for Companion Animals, he was so desperate for a new dog that he was undaunted by Harry's history. Just days before, he had lost his golden retriever, George, his constant companion for nine years. Charlie's grief knew no limits and the sight of this wiggling, licking, fat-footed yellow ball was irresistible. When he left the pound carrying the writhing pup, he was told that if he brought the dog back, the dog would have to be put down. Dogs only had three chances to be accepted into a family.

The minute Charlie arrived home with the puppy, his wife, Barbara, was not as charmed. I received a call asking us to bring our dog crate to their house. They needed something to contain the animal. When I arrived at their house with the crate, Barbara was considering getting into the crate herself. Seeing the whirling dervish racing around the living room, one could understand why she might be thinking that way. He had a tail that resembled that of an otter and if it hit you, you felt a nasty sting. When it hit the coffee table, all breakable items broke. Yes, Harry needed the crate and badly.

A month later Charlie and Barbara went on a two-week cruise. My husband and I said we would take Harry for that time because he was an unlikely kennel candidate. For the next two weeks we immersed ourselves full-time with Harry.

The first thing we learned was that he had temper tantrums if he was asked to do something he did not want to do. He would make eye contact with the demanding human and bark and bark in his or her face, making the most of eye contact. If you had never had a dog, you might have thought that this was intimidating or threatening. However, there was something about Harry that resembled a two-year old child, not a threatening dog. When he had one of these tantrums, we learned to ignore him for a couple of minutes and then go back to the original command. It always surprised him that his fit had not changed our minds. Just to show us that he needed to have a little say about his life, he would look up, give one "arf," and then do exactly what had been requested in the first place.

The second thing we learned was that he had no awareness of where his tail and back end were or what they were doing. Since he obviously had no control of this lethal weapon attached to his hind end, it was our responsibility to keep our eyes on it to minimize personal and/or property damage.

Once we all came to an understanding about his antics, they continued but with less intensity, and he became a bit more disciplined. Maybe we were just more observant. When he was overactive in the house, my husband would put him on a leash and march him around the living room, shouting "heel," "sit," "down," etc. Harry just loved it. It was a great game. He wagged his tail as he obeyed each command. The two weeks passed rapidly. This 50-pounder always had a cheerful disposition. He was no pouter. Harry just wanted (and needed) constant activity and entertainment.

He loved to get up on my lap, especially if he saw me reading the newspaper. He made sure that the paper did not cover my eyes because it was eyes where his communication skills were best developed. When Charlie and Barbara came home from their trip, we were sorry to see him go, but it was good to have time to catch up on other parts of our lives.

Through the next year, Harry grew to be an immense, muscular dog. He weighed 100 pounds and looked like he might be sneaking steroids. He loved to have overnights at our house. He never quite learned to heal on a leash, but that was not a bit surprising. He was always overwrought with excitement when he came and equally so when he went home with his family.

When Charlie and Barbara went to the lake each summer, we often visited them. A long, winding, forested lane led to their cabin. Harry's hearing was very acute and he seemed to know the sound of our car. Barbara said he would start running around the house in excitement when we turned into the little lane that was at least two blocks long. By the time we got to the house, he had not spent himself. Indeed, he was in a true frenzy. He could not help himself from jumping up on us, and of course his nose dug deep into my purse because he could always count on finding milk bones at the bottom.

Once we were in the house, he developed a ritual that he did for years. First, he scoured the house for gifts to bring us. He invariably started by bringing us a pillow from the couch. Next, it was usually a shoe, slipper, or sock, never all three. Sometimes, a magazine caught his fancy. His most creative gift was the fly swatter. Throughout the gift ceremony, his whole body wagged with joy. Finally, he always jumped up on my lap, just as he had when he was a puppy, only now he weighed over 100 pounds.

He loved the lake. The beach was sandy and the water was no more than shoulder high so we often just floated around in an inner tube, talking. Because Harry was a devotee of constant motion, he would stand up on his hind legs, put his front paws on my inner tube, and push me around the lake with his tail slashing through the water.

Some years later Barbara and Charlie

moved to Venice, Florida. When they planned to go to Europe, we volunteered to come to Florida and watch the house and Harry while they were gone. All of the human/dog bonding research says that if you bond with a dog when the dog is five months of age, he will never forget you. Well, we were about to put the research findings to the test. We had not seen Harry for almost three years when we flew to Florida. When we arrived at the house, Harry was out having a pedicure so he was not at home. Later, Charlie brought him home. When Harry walked in the living room, he walked right past me without looking in my direction. He spotted my husband and after a moment's hesitation, he wagged his tail and greeted him with great enthusiasm. Then he turned and looked at me. His tail stopped moving, he looked me in the eye and obviously said, "Gosh, is that really you?" He jumped up on my lap, put his head down, and closed his eyes.

We had a wonderful time in Venice, going to the off-leash dog beach, taking night walks, and of course having snacks. We even took him to Orlando for an overnight with friends who have a Shih Tsu. The two dogs got along famously, sharing food bowls and doing a lot of sniffing of each other. We were truly happy to have found Harry just the same loving friend as we had remembered him. It was a wonderful visit, but I do not know who looked sadder—my husband, me, or Harry when we left his house to return to Minnesota. He knew. We had our suitcases. We went home understanding why Charlie and so many other people cannot live without a pet.

The Weimaraner has made William Wegman famous

Dogs in the Business World

On the shore of beautiful Lake Tekapo in New Zealand stands a bronze statue of a sheep dog. It was commissioned on March 7, 1968, as a tribute to the contribution made by working collies to the economy of the area. It all began in 1855 when James Mackenzie, a Scottish shepherd turned sheep stealer and his dog, Friday, took control of thousands of sheep in the area. It is said that even after Mackenzie was apprehended, Friday kept moving his sheep. Eventually the dog was apprehended also, but the sheep farms continued to be successful in this difficult terrain because of the working collies. These collies represent but one very important way a dog can contribute to a man's economic betterment.

WEGMAN AND HIS WEIMARANERS

Not many people could distinguish a Weimaraner from a wiener dog before William Wegman dressed up his dogs to the joy of dog-lovers. Wegman, a talented artist, turned to photography in the early days of video. The words he puts in his dogs' mouths and the clothes he has his dogs wear just seem to suit the breed. When human hands instead of paws come out of sleeves cutting up potatoes in video and posing on calendars and posters, these straight-faced dogs seem believable whether dressed as drag queens or housewives making alphabet soup. Photographs of Wegman's dogs have been exhibited in many art museums and galleries in both the United States and Europe.

Man Ray, Wegman's first Weimaraner, was his business partner for almost twelve years. Then came Fay Ray, followed by her kids Batty, Chundo, and Crooky. A recent advertisement for Crypton® Fabrics pictures five wrinkly Wegman Weimaraner puppies assuring us that the blood line is being perpetuated.

Weimaraners have a sleek coat and come in all shades of gray, and as Wegman says, "Everyone knows that gray goes with anything." The dogs have a certain regal stature, and their curious pinkish noses seem to suggest a genuine hauteur that gives an additional comic twist to their acts. Since they are intelligent dogs, I imagine that behind their beautiful amber eyes they are laughing at the antics Wegman asks them to perform. Whether playing cards, gambling, writing letters, or making fashion statements, they convey a lot of whacky fun that never ceases to entertain their fans.

You could almost say that Wegman is dog-made. His business associates, Man Ray, Fay Ray, Batty, Chundo, Crooky, and their next generations are the perfect mimes for Wegman's whimsy, humor, dog training skill, and photographic talents. This is truly a unique canine/artist corporate enterprise.

ANZENBERGER AND PECORINO

On the cover of the March 2006 issue of the *Smithsonion* magazine sits a dog outside the gates of the Schoenbrunn Castle in Vienna, Austria. You cannot see his face, but you know he is in "shock and awe," just as I was the first time I saw this opulent edifice. Why is this stunning large white dog with black ears sightseeing?

It turns out he is not sightseeing; he is working with his collaborator, Toni Anzenberger, a young landscape photographer whose home is in Vienna. Mr. Anzenberger travels a great deal in his work and not too long ago on a visit to a farm in Verona, Italy, he learned that someone had a spotted puppy with black ears that no one wanted. He saw the puppy and decided to

The photogenic Pecorino

adopt him. Because the puppy looked like a little sheep, he named him Pecorino, the word for "little sheep" in Italian, or so Anzenberger thought. It turned out that *Pecorino* is a kind of cheese. It did not matter to the puppy because he was learning German, not Italian, so he kept the name, Pecorino.

When the dog got a little older, Anzenberger took him on an assignment in Tuscany. Mr. Anzenberger started to regret this decision because the dog kept running in front of the camera just as he pressed the shutter of the camera. He did not intend to have his dog in his pictures, but he soon discovered that the pictures with Pecorino in them took on a special character so he made the dog a partner in his professional work. The two now travel together throughout Europe. They have become globe-trotters, going to Paris, London, Greece, Barcelona, and Munich, just to mention a few destinations.

Anyone who has ever tried to travel with a pet can certainly imagine what this photographer has had to go through. Some countries were closed to animals, some were slow to open their doors, and a few opened their borders wide. For instance, England and Scandinavia require months of waiting to assure that a dog does not have rabies before entering the country. In Lisbon, they were escorted off a "no dogs" train. However, as Pecorino's name became well known, they were given some special privileges (such as taking over a double-decker bus for a shoot in London). In this particular picture, Pecorino is standing on his hind legs with his front paws and head sticking out the upper deck window looking down and slightly acrophobic. He has even posed sitting on the red velvet seats of a German opera house.

According to Mr. Anzenberger, Pecorino usually strikes his own poses. As a result, the camera has to be always ready to catch some of the special moments, such as a close-up of Pecorino smelling a large bunch of purple grapes. When you look at this picture, you can see that Pecorino has selected just the right grape for his kind of wine. He has the satisfied look of a wine connoisseur sniffing his favorite aged vintage.

This talented pair continues to travel by car because neither one likes to fly. At art shows, the artist can pretty much go unrecognized but not Pecorino. He will lie near their works and accept belly rubs until closing time. Along with other artists, they have a gallery, Anzenberger Gallery in Austria, and a business where you can order color photos, postcards, annual wall calendars and some of their books. Go to www.anzenbergergallery.com and enjoy.

RIN TIN TIN, A HOLLYWOOD ACTOR

One of the first Hollywood canine actors (before Asta, Lassie, and Toto) was Rin Tin Tin, a German shepherd. Just before the end of WWI, on September 15, 1918, an American sergeant, Lee Duncan, rescued a shell-shocked puppy from a bombed-out dog kennel in Lorraine, France. He named him for Rintintin, a puppet that French children gave to American soldiers for good luck. At the end of the war two months later, Duncan brought "Rinty," as he now called him, to his home in Los Angeles, California.

Duncan trained his dog to do tricks and showed him in several dog shows. Darryl Zanuck, the well-known film producer, happened to be at one of these dog shows where Duncan had Rinty performing tricks and jumping to great heights. Zanuck hired Rinty for his movies. In his first job he played a wolf in a movie, and later on he played a valiant dog in over fifteen movies. The success of Rin Tin Tin movies was ultimately credited with saving Warner Brothers from bankruptcy.

As a celebrity, Rin Tin Tin ate steak prepared daily by a private chef. He was also given a star on the Hollywood Walk of Fame, and even after the dog's death, there has been a steady stream of books, television shows, and more movies showing his extraordinary acting in many adventure stories.

Rinty died on August 8, 1932. Duncan took his body back to France where he had been born. Rin Tin Tin is buried at the Cimetiére des Chiens, a renowned pet cemetery in a Paris suburb. It is truly remarkable to note that this famous dog lives on through a 103-year continuous bloodline that is maintained at a kennel in Latexo, Texas.

*Bubba,
Rin Tin Tin VII*

STEVIE, A HOTEL MASCOT

For several years, Chicago's Monaco Hotel had a canine public relations assistant. The hotel had already shown that it was a dog-friendly hotel where canines received a special bed and a bowl. The beginning of having a canine staff member all started when Meredith Voller, associate director of sales, rescued a quivering ten-month-old Lhasa Apso from a Humane Society in Gary, Indiana.

She brought the little dog to her home and named her Stevie Nix. With love and kindness, Stevie began to be less afraid of strangers and started enjoying her new home, but she was lonesome when Meredith went off to work. Because Meredith had toyed with the idea of a hotel mascot, she proposed the idea to the hotel manager. They agreed to try it. They would give Stevie a one-year probation, time to learn good manners and get used to strangers, both human and canine. She had some obedience training, learned to walk well on leash to and from their home, and got used to being petted by strangers. As a shy pup, she went from being reluctant to letting strangers pet her to thinking it was her due.

Stevie's probationary period went well, although there were a few special things that needed emphasizing like an attitude toward

Stevie, the hotel mascot

men's shoes. Stevie mixed well with hotel guests, became especially popular with children, and got along with both dogs and cats. When the job got a little too hectic, she flopped down for a nap with her rag doll and rawhide under Voller's desk.

Stevie established quite a reputation. She was on "Good Morning America," went on speaking engagements for animal shelters, and went to personnel meetings. She sometimes even accompanied her boss when there was a dissatisfied customer. Her very presence always eased the situation. During Stevie's work life, there was no doubt that she was very good for business.

Sadie

Sadie

A Little Sniffer for the Beagle Brigade

Dog owners know a lot about sniffing. Just keeping a pet's head up during a walk is a real challenge, and is almost impossible if that dog happens to be some kind of a retriever. Dogs have 220 million scent receptors compared to 5 million scent receptors in humans. This extraordinary olfactory sense is why dogs have so much fun smelling things and why they can smell a lot more information about their environment than any human can. Besides your everyday neighborhood sniffing dog, there are professional sniffers: K-9 police dogs; search and rescue dogs used in fires, earthquakes, and disasters; and search dogs used for the detection of bombs, drugs, and arson. These professionals, usually German shepherds, golden and Labrador retrievers, or border collies, are impressive in size and have large noses.

In contrast, the Beagle Brigade uses little sniffers. These little beagles protect American agriculture, working for the U.S. Department of Agriculture Animal and Plant Health Inspection Service. Hal Fingerman founded the Beagle Brigade in 1984 at the Los Angeles airport for the purpose of reducing the number of diseased and toxic plants coming into the United States from other countries. Agricultural diseases were entering the United States because the system of random searches of baggage was not adequate.

Fingerman originally preferred beagles for the detection of plant diseases because they not only have good noses but because they are small, friendly, and not threatening to people. Indeed, beagles can detect and identify smells so faint that even scientific equipment cannot detect.

Brigade dogs come from shelters, rescue groups, or donations by owners. Jackpot 1 was one of the Brigade's first and finest detectors. There are pictures of Jackpot 1 sitting with her contraband of one day at J.F.K. airport in New York. There are piles of grapes, mangos, pears, beans, and various meats. Identifying one hundred pounds of various foods a day was not unusual for this dog.

Sadie, a charming little ten-month-old beagle was rescued from a Florida shelter for Brigade training in 1997. She was paired with Irene, a PPQ (Plant Protection and Quarantine) officer. It was pretty much love at first sight for both of them and that love lasted throughout Sadie's life.

Together, they started training at the USDA's National Detector Dog Training Center in Orlando, Florida. The Center is located on a large parcel of land, has many dog kennels, several quarantine runs, simulations of postal and passenger arrival areas, and typical classrooms. Sadie enjoyed her training. She was playful and loved to search out smells with her partner. Some dogs have to leave the program because they become agitated by the sound of a crying child, a luggage carousel starting up, the sound of a jet engine, or just the hubbub of a busy airport. Sadie might look up to find the source of such sounds, but they never deterred her from her task.

Sadie graduated with top grades. She learned to identify the core group of five odors: pork, beef, mango, citrus fruits, and apple. After graduation Irene taught her to recognize more scents on the job. A very good beagle may eventually learn to recognize up to 50 different smells. Sadie learned almost 45 smells before she retired. When a forbidden scent was recognized, Sadie learned to sit next to the piece of luggage or package and wait for a little reward from Irene as she inspected the suspicious item. These are the moments that the game is most fun. At graduation Sadie received the Brigade's uniform, a distinctive green coat that reads "Agriculture's Beagle Brigade" on one side and "Protecting American Agriculture" on the other side.

Irene and Sadie were assigned to the Miami airport. The Beagle Brigade works at many major airports where there are incoming international flights, at U.S. post offices receiving international mail, and at some border crossings. It is estimated that on average, the Brigade keeps over 75,000 prohibited products from entering the country a year.

Because of the importance of their sensitivity to the smell of foods, Beagle Brigade dogs live in kennels rather than the home of their partner. Sadie's work day started when Irene picked her up at the kennel and drove her to the airport. They usually examined the baggage of international travelers for about six flights each day, trying to take a twenty minute rest for each work hour. Some days they went to an area school to demonstrate Sadie's keen nose for the children. Sadie's tail always wagged "Thank you" when the children clapped. A beagle's work career lasts about six to eight years. Sadie worked diligently for eight years. When she retired, Irene adopted her and she lived with Irene's loving family until she died four years later.

These spunky little fun-loving dogs have been the first line of defense against contamination of our country's food, plants, and agricultural products. The Beagle Brigade has twice been awarded special recognition by the Port Authority of New York and New Jersey as airport ambassadors for outstanding customer service. The Pedigree All Star Hall of Fame inducted them into the National Dog Museum in St. Louis, Missouri, as the outstanding service program in 1993. After the tragedy of

September 11, the Brigade became a part of the Department of Homeland Security. We all owe a debt of gratitude to these little dogs, our agricultural border patrol.

Mark and Tyke

Mark & Tyke

Canine Police Partners

If you had walked past my neighbor's back-yard on St. Paul's Grand Avenue a few years ago, you would have seen Tyke, a beautiful German shepherd playing catch with Mark and Linda's three children, Angela, Daniel, and Brian. What a happy family pet! Yes, he was that, but this dog was a great deal more than a pet. Tyke was a highly trained and competent member of the St. Paul Police Canine Unit, one of the outstanding canine units in the United States. He went to work with his partner, Officer Mark Ficcadenti, for nine years.

Tyke first went through the twelve-week training period that is required before a dog and partner can start patrolling the streets together. To be eligible for this rigorous training, a dog must be bred for such work. These dogs used to come from the United States and were often donated to the Canine Unit by a breeder or an owner. However, over the past decade, U.S. bred German shepherds have lost some of the aggressiveness necessary to join a police force. Therefore, today most of the dogs come from Europe, usually Germany, the Czech Republic, or Belgium and cost at least $6,000. Tyke was among the last to come from the United States. He was donated to the Canine Unit by a couple in St. Paul. They enjoyed keeping track of their gift through Mark who often sent them pictures and reports of this remarkable dog.

Tyke started training when he was just one year old. Basic training is rigorous and often grueling. Both dog and handler must be in excellent physical condition to endure the running, repetitious maneuvers, and often bad weather, wet, cold or hot. Handlers lose weight while dogs learn to climb ladders, walk over planks from heights, and stay calm when they hear gun fire. They also learn tracking, building searches, handler protection, criminal apprehension, and obedience for both attack and release of an assailant. In addition, some dogs are cross-trained for bomb and/or drug discovery. At the end of the 12-week training, dogs and partners demonstrate their skills at a graduation ceremony. My heart stands still every time I see one of these dogs leap through an open car window to attack a perpetrator, just one of the capabilities demonstrated at each graduation.

Mark has been a trainer for sixteen years and the Head Trainer at the Timothy J. Jones Canine Training Facility for five years. Training has many facets. First, assessing the personality of the handler in training and judging the dog's personality is basic to successful outcomes. The ability to do this comes from experience, intuition, and training. Mark says that sometimes it is harder to teach the handler than it is to teach the dog. (I observed the same phenomenon when I took our golden retriever to obedience classes.) When graduation comes, each pair has an opportunity to show evidence of their hard-earned skills. After graduation, they go out together and do what is known as "patrol learning," learning from experience in unsafe and often very dangerous situations.

Through the years, Tyke and Mark "got their man" hundreds of times. Sometimes the apprehension was easier than other times. A few memorable incidents are particularly illustrative of this particular dog's intelligence and training.

One night, while out on patrol, Mark and Tyke were called to a robbery where an off-duty deputy had been repeatedly shot. The assailant had gotten away and an intense hunt was initiated. Mark and Tyke inspected an area where there were few lights. As they searched for evidence, Tyke suddenly came to attention close to some bushes. Using his flashlight, Mark examined the area and found a gun that had been thrown into the bushes. Mark brought the gun to the police lab. When it was examined, the bullet that had hit the deputy matched the gun and the fingerprints on the gun led to the arrest of the offender.

On another occasion, Mark and Tyke were called because the security alarm at Dayton's Department store in downtown St. Paul had been going off for several nights. No one knew if it was due to an electrical short or if there were intruders. Several searches had led to no findings so it seemed quite possible that these were false alarms. At 1:30 A.M. one night, Mark and Tyke were on duty when the Dayton's alarm went off again. With one other team, Mark and Tyke started a search of the building. Having found nothing on the first three floors, Mark and Tyke started their search of the fourth floor. They started in some dressing rooms and traversed the entire floor. Finding nothing, Mark said to Tyke, "Let's get out of here. There's nothing here." They retraced their tracks as they left, but this time Tyke led Mark back into one of the dressing rooms. Tyke sat down and put his nose up in the air, sniffing and looking upward. Mark looked up at the ceiling and saw a space between two of the ceiling tiles. At that very moment, a large man jumped down onto both of them. Both Mark and Tyke struggled. The man was not only large but very strong. Finally Tyke managed to wiggle free. Tyke fiercely grabbed the man's arm until Mark was finally able to get out his handcuffs and subdue the man. While these dogs are trained to attack when commanded, they need no command when they see their partner in trouble.

On yet another occasion while Mark and

Tyke were patrolling on John Ireland Boulevard on July 5th at 1:00 A.M., Mark got a call from another officer nearby at the White Castle restaurant saying he was hearing gun shots. "Are you sure you are not hearing the fireworks from the Taste of Minnesota?" asked Mark. "No, these are definitely gun shots," answered the other officer. Mark started driving toward the houses where the shots seemed to come. He stopped his car and turned on his spot light. He thought he could make out a man behind a tree. He got out and, using the car for cover, watched the man come toward him with an assault rifle. Next, the man threw the rifle on the ground and Mark held his gun on him. Suddenly several people came out of a house and one shouted, "He just killed my girl-friend." Four or five men tried to wrestle the man but he overpowered them and started to run away. Seeing what was happening and without command, Tyke jumped out of the open car door and gave chase. Tyke attacked the man and brought him under control for Mark to make the arrest. Suddenly, more terrified people came running out of the house. The man had gone on a shooting spree in the house just minutes before. He had killed two people inside the house before running out of ammunition for his Russian SKS rifle.

When Tyke was four years old, he was diagnosed with a mild neurological degenerative disease, but he worked capably until he retired from his work when he was ten years old. He lived out his next three years as the family pet, which of course he had been all along.

When Tyke retired, Mark got a new partner, Shadow. Shadow had an entirely different temperament. He was aloof with people and ignored them, but he could become aggressive if someone invaded his space. However, unlike Tyke, he accepted other dogs. In other words, he was just the opposite of Tyke.

Shadow's bond was with Mark and no one else. Therefore, Shadow lived outside their home while Tyke lived inside. When Mark would practice commands with Shadow in the yard, Tyke often watched through a window and carried out the same commands inside the house.

Mark's wife, Linda, did not like having a dog that was so aloof. So after Tyke died, she decided to try a few innovative interventions to try to make Shadow more friendly. Looking Shadow in the eye seemed to agitate him, so Linda decided to go outside and sit with her back to the dog. She talked to him. The conversation might be about her feelings for him, about politics, adventures of the children who were now grown and living elsewhere, or what she and Mark would have for dinner. Gradually, Shadow got used to her presence and to her voice. As time went on, when the dog let her pet him, she gave him a treat.

At last, they became friends and Shadow now lets her nuzzle him the way an ordinary pet would do. Without the children at home, the family is smaller, but it is now complete with a canine police dog who has also become a full family member.